ACTIVE SPORTS Hiking

Published by Creative Education

P.O. Box 227, Mankato, Minnesota 56002

Creative Education is an imprint of The Creative Company

www.thecreativecompany.us

Design by Blue Design

Production by The Design Lab

Printed in the United States of America

Photographs by Alamy (Danita Delimont), Corbis (Tony West), Dreamstime (Amygdalaimagery, Kapu), Getty Images (Raymond Gehman, Bill Hatcher, Dave Schiefelbein), iStockphoto (Xavi Arnau, Ben Blankenburg, Waylon Brinck, David Ciemny, Carol Gering, Dave Hughes, Gene Lee, Richard Mirro, Doug Schneider)

Library of Congress Cataloging-in-Publication Data

Bodden, Valerie.

Hiking / by Valerie Bodden.

p. cm. — (Active sports)

Includes index.

ISBN 978-1-58341-698-3

1. Hiking—Juvenile literature. I. Title. II. Series.

GV199.52.B63 2009

796.51—dc22   2007045823

First Edition

9 8 7 6 5 4 3 2 1

Hiking

Valerie Bodden

CREATIVE EDUCATION

Sometimes hikers have to cross a creek or stream.

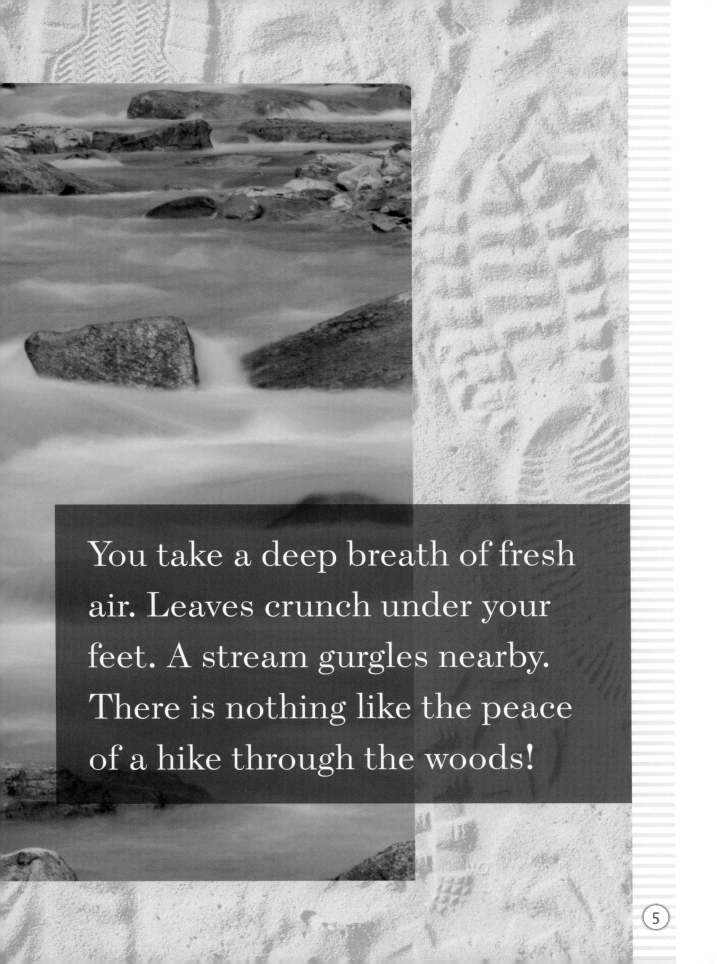

You take a deep breath of fresh air. Leaves crunch under your feet. A stream gurgles nearby. There is nothing like the peace of a hike through the woods!

It takes about 30 minutes to hike one mile (1.6 km).

Hiking means taking a long walk outside. Lots of people like to hike. Some people hike alone. They are called solo hikers. Other people hike with friends.

Most trails are marked with signs to show the way.

Most hikers follow a **trail**. Some trails are easy. They are good for new hikers. Other trails are hard. They might go through **mountains**. The trails can be very long. The longest trail in the United States is called the Pacific Crest Trail. It is 2,650 miles (4,265 km) long!

Hikers try to "wear in" new boots before hiking.

Most hikers wear hiking boots. The boots are strong. They have deep **grooves** on the bottom. The grooves help keep hikers from slipping.

Most hikers carry a backpack. They put food and water in the backpack. Hikers carry a compass and a topographic (*top-uh-GRAF-ick*) map, too. The compass shows what way they are going. The map shows things like rivers and hills.

Some hikers use walking sticks to help them balance.

Some hikers take day hikes. These hikes take only one to eight hours. Other hikers camp overnight. These hikers are called backpackers. Backpackers carry a tent and sleeping bag in their backpack.

Backpackers need to take everything they might need.

Big backpacks have lots of pockets for hiking gear.

Hikers have to be careful. They have to watch out for animals such as bears. They have to know what to do if someone gets hurt. Hikers should always carry a **first aid kit** with them.

Some trails start and end in the same place.

Hikers have to make sure to stay on the trail. If they go off the trail, they could get lost. If hikers get lost, they stop and stay where they are. They blow a whistle to help people find them.

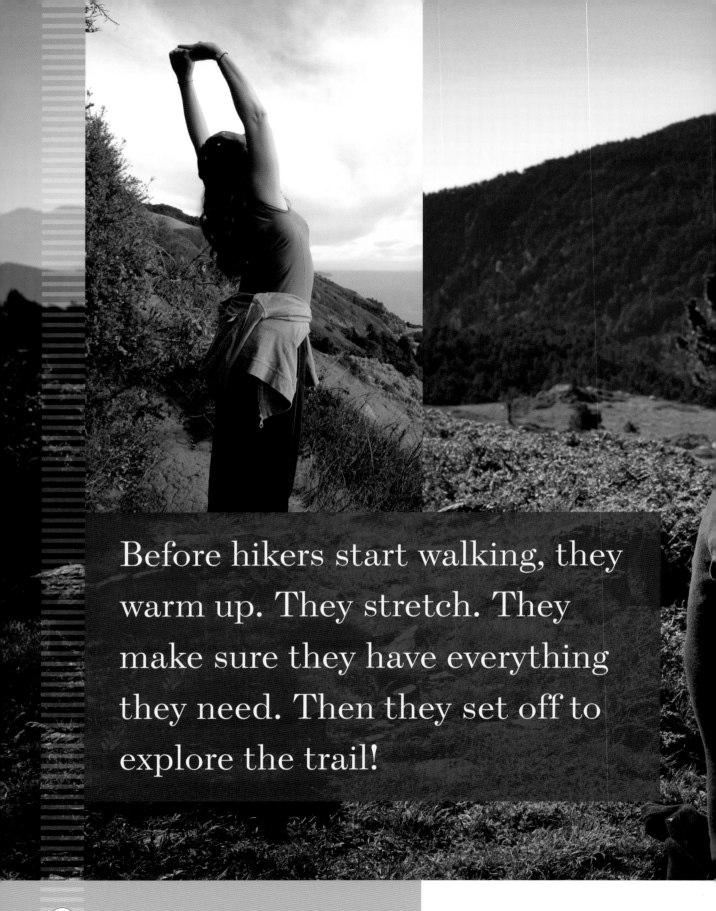

Before hikers start walking, they warm up. They stretch. They make sure they have everything they need. Then they set off to explore the trail!

Hikers need to take plenty of water breaks.

Zigzagging up hills can make them easier to climb.

GLOSSARY

first aid kit—a small box filled with bandages and other things that might be needed if someone gets hurt

grooves—long, narrow holes

mountains—very big hills made of rock

trail—a path through a wild area

INDEX